THEN AND NOW

THEN AND NOW

JANETTE PIELOOR

RECENT
WORK
PRESS

Then and Now
Recent Work Press
Canberra, Australia

Copyright © Janette Pieloor, 2019

ISBN: 9780648404293 (paperback)

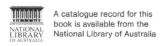
A catalogue record for this
book is available from the
National Library of Australia

All rights reserved. This book is copyright. Except for private study, research, criticism or reviews as permitted under the Copyright Act, no part of this book may be reproduced, stored in a retrieval system, or transmitted in any form by any means without prior written permission. Enquiries should be addressed to the publisher.

Cover design: Peter Pieloor
Set by Charlotte Anderson

recentworkpress.com

Contents

You are invited	1
Moon	2
Old Egg	3
If it were Saturday ...	4
Mimicry	5
My father's words	6
Sea days	7
Suitcase	8
Shape shifters	9
Ceremony	10
My whisperer	11
His noble absence	12
Your choice	13
Telling him	14
A second time	15
Revolving doors	16
Lonely hearts	17
Tentacles	18
His parallel universe	19
Muscles	20
You weren't available	21
Love letters	22
I didn't know	23
Ghost	24
Borrowed	25
Silent in her waiting	26
It's time	27
Sea	28
Heartbeat	29
My Jack-in-the box	30
White elephant	32
Welcome to my life	33
The meanwhile living	34
Loneliness	35

The day my heart became a bird	36
Soon	37
She's here again	38
Polaroid	39
Mr Gusto	40
Hats	42
Happiness	43
One room	44
Not alone	45
Remember	46
Her rose	47
Hands	48
Next	49
The gaps between	50
Tiny room	51
Empty clothes-hangers	52
White	53
Dew-drop whispering	54
Little face frightened	55
Loss of her	56
Holding places	57
Your turn	58
waiting	59
Light	60
Then and now	61

You are invited

It's the large house with the long, polished
hall and veranda half-way around, the one
with the green frog who lives in the letterbox.

You will see the cousins and parents arrive,
parcels being unpacked, grown-ups talking
over tea.

You can come with us to the beach, sit under
big umbrellas, watch the lifesavers legs-up
on the sand, wear swimmers striped and salty.

You can watch the big crabs the uncles caught
change colour in the boiling copper, see Nanna
chop off the old hen's head, smell Pa's pipe.

You can play under the ripe fruit trees beside
the chicken run, roll along the thick grass, climb
the old fig tree, eat mangoes until you itch.

At night, you can creep into Nana's kitchen,
giggle if her ginger beer pops, spy the Christmas
pudding full of sixpences hanging in its balloon.

You will leave your sandals outside, find a bunk,
talk and tease with the cousins, listen to the beat
of sea, sleep under a green mosquito net.

When you wake up, you will dress in your best,
swap lollies wrapped in coloured paper, shake
the parcels under the tree.

You will smell the roast, see the white linen spread
on the long table, listen to the grown-ups' stories.
You can come again, if you like.

Moon

My mother comes to me
with a smile and an egg in her hand;
places it in my palm, shows me how
to crack its orange shell, unfold
its rubbery overcoat, reveal
a tiny soft ball, we name Moon.

In a soft voice, just for me,
my mother explains how Moon
and I will always be
part of each other, in a shared journey
to womanhood: a rhythm
Moon controls.

Old Egg

Big Egg, do you remember
Nanna weaving you into
our stories we made up?

Nanna holding my hand
at dusk to first meet you –
a magic, floating egg yolk?

Walking with us, pacing us
on your invisible long legs;
first one side, then the other?

Playing hide-and-seek
behind the old plane trees
lacing our street?

......

Old Egg, tonight Nanna's
back, holding my hand –
we're singing Humpty Dumpty again!

If it were Saturday ...

I'll get dressed-up, go next door to Hilda's shop, sit on
its steps, eat a bun while she keeps an eye on me. I'll
go through the back door, walk along the boards to the
Bakehouse, to find Jim and watch him knead the dough;
slide out the steaming loaves on long, wooden spatulas.

I'll draw on the dry dirt with sticks from the bush behind
our grey back gate, and if the Aborigines are in town,
I'll listen to their murmuring under the gum trees and wait
for the women in floral dresses to bring their blackened
billies for water from our tank; walk with them each way.

My sister will join me on our board and rope swings,
we'll make a cubby-house for our things, and if our
father has trimmed the pepper-trees, we'll stack the
branches, slide their leaves across our noses; to later
hear our mother tell us we have pepper faces.

Mimicry

My sister and I wheel our babies around the yard
in cane prams, stop by our little wooden house
with its morning glory vine, hold a bottle to each
open mouth and whisper to each other.

With soft murmuring we rock our babies in yellow
painted bassinettes draped with mosquito nets,
cross-stitched around their edges; then dress
and wrap them in hand-made clothes and covers.

We tuck the babies in to sleep so we can have
tea in tiny blue and white cups and saucers, then
climb onto our swings, swing as high as we dare
until our mother calls us inside.

My father's words

He had boy words for his copper pennies
rolled and knuckles swapped; happy words
for silver sixpences found in Christmas
puddings.

He had gentle words for his stepmother
when they stood at the mantelpiece in her
little house; his elbow resting on its polished
surface, hers on her crocheted linen cloth.

His *easy* words: "Bloody Australian" were
known as wicked by Auntie, who wore soft
coloured hand-knitted cardigans; mourned
for her soldier fiancée.

Sometimes I see an unknown grandfather's
ghost standing beside his grandchild or hear
him singing *Danny Boy* in an Irish pub's
floating fug.

Sometimes I think I hear his loving father
words, just for me.

Sea days

Sea spins quick-turn
bursting boys
teasing smooth-bean
long-legged girls
threading milk-
starfish dreams.

Sea, boasting
swells and sings
to prude-green
cloud-frilled hills
that will wait
the turning of the years.

Suitcase

Who hung that misty banner?
'To the city...Country wings must fly'

The suitcase she gave me on a step and train
turning me away from her; one last longing
girling look to catch her eye, to call across
the platform *'I'm not sure I believe in God'*
and see a plinth in stockinged shoes, smiling
proudly up for a daughter.

On the train, riven from those country
faces and familiar lanes that led to each
house-front's welcome for a first-name;
from my home, its clopping gate, chipped
path, welcoming steps, up into its polished
proud hall, to call out *'it's me.'*

Delivered to a city's unknown rhythms:
that large brown leather suitcase and
buckled strap carrying the years through
doors, into boarding houses, attics, shared
rooms.

Always remembered she and I on that loud
platform, her gift of letting go, I still unwrap
and hold.

Shape shifters

Quietly, in the soft drizzle of early morning,
a mob appears on the sloped hill as if in
a slow movie, their dark eyes watching
below antenna ears.

When full sun arrives, they turn in unison
to face its globe; a thin gold line outlines
their bodies in the stillness.

Long necks patrol their turf as they feed
on its glittering moist grasses amongst
the swabbed shrubs, their fur changing
colour as they become sun's shadow catchers.

Silently they hunker down, folding
their heavy haunches, hiding the soft creams
of their underbellies; they are darkened mounds,
weighing readiness for propulsion; a balance
of springs that sense earth.

They are shape shifters: tall, patient
rabbits in bibbed aprons; large pears on
sticks; full clean slugs when lying at rest;
their muscled tails, pythons in the grass.

Ceremony

Winter has exposed the old white, wooden
hives untidily stacked behind our dividing
bushes, and we smell honey.

We see him, a man of few words, standing
on the road, rubbing his ear with his finger,
watching his bees swarming and pleating along
an old tree branch, layering and fizzing it
with their bodies.

He must know there is a princess-in-waiting,
hidden among them.
He must be quick.

He comes with a wooden ladder, an old rake
and a cardboard packing box with honey inside.
He's wearing *astronaut* head gear and his hands
are in purple washing-up gloves.

The dogs are quiet, the air humid and still,
and the children across the road
watch from the verge.

He shakes the branch, guides the rake,
layers the bees into the box, their dark
bodies piping, pasting its sides.

She has accepted him; will be crowned.

My whisperer

Sea
you find me
sound slap me
thrill me
in the froth and curl of you

                  in the sting of you
                  I tongue your salt
                  you push me down
                  in your feral boast
                  to your waiting sand

you raise me up
to float in you
we hold hands
I lie in you –
my susurrus

                  your waves know
                  my body
                  knew my
                  flailing arms
                  you are my
                  birth memory

His noble absence

I held him close, his warm body
in dependency.

I could have left with him, in my arms.
He would have lived one more day for me
but I chose the unforgiving present.

I held him for a little longer, weighing
what left my arms, an absence in form,
a weightless shape of what had been,
shared, given.

I see his ghost sometimes in house
windows and in yards. He'll pause
when I pass, shivering me a light,
following me into our past.

I wish that I too might have
such a noble absence
when it is my time.

Your choice

You left with the clock, sand timer
and gold watch, though I asked if I
could keep them to lighten your load.

You said my suitcase was too small.

What else did you put in yours? How
did you know when it was time? Did
Time make a bargain with you?

What will you do with your memories?
Forgetting, a task you never mastered
and forgiving, your noose.

It was your choice but you left me your
story to unpack; it doesn't fit into my
suitcase.

Telling him

I want to be in that sticky place
between the two doors –
      the before and after,
      take my time.

Move on, don't stay too long, don't
      get stuck, my son replied.

I reminded him he cries in movies.

He gave me his parting words:
      there is only one thing certain –
      time changes everything.
I was happy with that.

A second time

I still slide out the second drawer
before I remember
you don't have the top one anymore.

Sign this   then sign this.
I still love you   but.

There were no words   before.
I couldn't talk to you   then.
I can't talk to you   now.

A large metal Santa's round red face
in a shopping trolley staring at me.
Nothing you can do!   I heard.

The cockatoo on the highest branch
of the old oak tree   leaning over
its beak pin-pricking me.
Nothing I can do!   I call.

I don't want your knowledge
you would say:

No reply needed
your flight plan.

Revolving doors

Before and after the noose/ Did I see him or was I told?/ A box in a shed to stand on?/ Hung nets sucking water from buckets/ Saving a baby in a heat wave/ A teaspoon of brandy on the sixth day/ Sign at the front gate/ Beware she bites/ A tantrum/ Not a flower-girl/ Dressing up/ Parading the house veranda/ Was it I who boasted a teenager running from the bull?/ A toddler at midnight left to talk herself out/ Refusing revolving doors/ Refusing the noose/

Lonely hearts

Your ad, my phone call, your invitation and I
was to ring the re-painted bell. I had passed
the first qualification on a dating checklist,
sugar-coated for reality's loneliness test:
understood, not spoken, was a possible
exit.

I rang that bell, smelt its fresh paint.
You quickly opened the door before I
could speak; your arms held out, you
danced on the balls of your feet,
turning and chanting *Will I do?*
Will I do?

When I stepped inside, you gave
me a glass of pink champagne,
explained you were once a
prize ballroom dancer.

In the turning point of us,
you offered me love and
bubbles: an image to
remember.

Tentacles

Boys that floated in the dark:
one from the concentration camp
who taught himself to walk again;
the other chosen to clean up the bodies
at the school, after the bombs.

Both with a darkness they didn't know
how to unlock.

Now, opaque old men with tentacles of age:
jellyfishes without sting, forever kept in a void,
caught in the tides of a before they couldn't
unlearn.

May the sun find you.

His parallel universe

He's looking for lazy cutlery to lunch with his parents;
last night's stand-up comedy dreams still in his head.
He lowers into his seat, tells them in punch-line
energy, he's too old to train for the mission to Mars,
though his back would like zero gravity.

He's taught his muscles a soft sit, knows and waits
for his imagined lighthouse to wink a shift of pain,
roll him waves. Bowl in hand, around he goes, eating
upright on a circular route from kitchen to family
room, lounge to dining room; the two at the table
soft eyeing him, waiting.

He's come to sit again to tell them about his parallel
universe. He'll walk with his father in the afternoons,
and each night, lying on his bed, read stories
on Skype to his children.

Muscles

You lie on the sand,
one eye looking at me.
I watch the adjustments
        your muscles make,
        see ripples and beads –
        no hook.
You flip into the water,
leave a silvery divergence:
cool in your skin now.
        I wait.

You weren't available

I rang to tell you it was my son's birthday today,
tell you I'd rung him early, a toll for that fat day
and how he was the first to be fitted into a father's
arms; how he was my alien. He reminds me *I say
this each year, at the exact time:* he always laughs
then, indulging me, but you weren't available.

I rang to tell you I'd treated myself to a sugar hit
coffee in a dim lit restaurant: I'd walked in as if
a heroine in a mystery novel, then sideways read
my book there as if it held secrets; that the couple
next to me popped champagne, asked me if I'd like
a glass. Of course I said yes, but wiped the rim first.

I rang to tell you I bought myself a chocolate bar,
that it melted on the way home, next to the chunky
meat pie from our favourite bakery; that when I got
back, handsome José came to aerosol those paper
wasps from the deck and throw their nest away,
that it made me sad, but you weren't available.

Love letters

I'm sharing a house with an older woman
I've tried to ignore her   but she's covered
all the mirrors
I've tried not to hear her   but she's clumsy
and noisy
I plan my exits   but she pops up
beside me

She's searching through   my stuff
thinks it's hers
She's on a quest   thinks I've hidden
love letters I wrote
thinks I'll want to listen   to her reading
all of them

Letters ... I hear her mumbling...
When someone   couldn't spell
commitment
When friends   drank all the wine

If she could forget I wrote them   I might make
a bargain with her

I didn't know

I didn't know
     in those last days
     when the house was packed up
     and you were leaving,

     when we unravelled
     our questions and answers
     and juggled
     our monologues
     around a marriage and children,

     when we revisited the houses we lived in,
     cities we moved to, mourned
     our animal companions.

I didn't know
     that I still loved you
     until old cat's green-glass eyes
     spiralled into mine.

     But you had already left.

Ghost

At the top of our hill, I hear her calling
'higher', hear her dancing feet tapping
up from the empty swing.

I feel her hand in mine, and we walk along
the bitumen path,
see a brown snake in the sun
glittering the edges of the grass,
take our short-cut past the sodden creek
where the fickle rains have wedged
and flattened the reeds.

She stays until we're at the corner house,
with its tinkling piano. I want to leave with her,
but never see where she goes.

Home is a welcoming nod from the young
blackwood we planted for her.

Borrowed

I was day-dreaming when they came:
first the curly blonde-haired girl, skipping
and spinning in a floral dress, telling
me, she is six and has brothers;
then two boys, leaning over my shoulders,
faces shining, chanting in turn:
I'm four!
I'm two!

And oh! I borrowed them:
We held hands. I took them to the zoo;
the park to roll on the grass and slide
the silver slides; the pool for a swim
and coloured ice-creams for after,
before they walked me home.

Some days I think I hear their laughter,
see their shining faces.

I always wanted grandchildren

Silent in her waiting

She hears my waking, has been waiting,
stretching into the spaces of herself,
acting out night's dream of the wild
but expecting my patting all the same.

She'll horse-march to her bowl, stand
upright above it: her ears she'll flicker,
tail hook-curl and soft beat the carpet;
watch me with clear glass eyes,
opening and slit-closing.

She'll wait while I unroll my morning
monologue, divvy up food.

I watch her elegantly eat; step away
from her empty bowl, without a paw
shake or meow. During the day, she'll
present for repeats and I'll be grateful
for the rhythm of her company.

It's time

Mother, will you be the translator
of the shadows revolving
of the two girls sleeping
behind the closed door?

Mother, what was it he said to you?
Did you tell me?
Would I have understood?

Mother, he closed your door too
to spin into another without you:
there were no shadow words
for the three of us!

Mother, you still have the memories
of before.
Will you share them now?
Am I grown up enough?

Mother, he took my memories with him.
I need them back.
How long do I have to wait?

There are grandchildren on the stairs.

Sea

I laid the sea on the floor
of my motel room
in those last days

I walked in my wet clothes
onto the old, wooden slat path
sprinkled with sand

It must have been
the seventh wave
that stole me

Sea in me
salt sating me
waves hugging me

Sea will say goodbye
spiral back into her wave
take my mother with her

I press down
to stop my feet
flying away

Heartbeat

She walks just like a duck in her old age
when she goes out, her neck held up between
her shoulder blades. She keeps her legs, one
in front of the other, to be sure-to be sure,
keeping heart's pace.

She feels its beat as if it's in each foot,
rhyming the present but bringing the past.
She hears the tap-tapping of her twenty-
year old self, strut-strutting behind her
in high-heeled shoes.

She's grateful for daily tasks she breathes
her life into and day-dreams that either
leaving or returning, she's always walking
home to her first heartbeat, just around
the corner.

My Jack-in-the box

From the beginning of Winter, I watched you;
first an antenna ear, then a delicate paw,
next a tiny face, in and out of your fur fort;
your mother's body balancing each time
you left or returned.

I watched you and your mother in gentle rains
and mists, feeding on moist glittering grasses
amongst the bush shrubs and with the other
steps and stairs of your family, you not far
from your mother.

My own children's first cubby house began at my
feet with cloths, pillows, boxes, toys and little
faces peering in and out, then whole bodies
disappearing and re-appearing in scattered
noise while I kept watch.

They grew as I watched them. When
the youngest called "Wait for me," trailing
the others' voices, then turning to me with
a proud smile, I knew it was his turn, his
feet to noise on the steps leading outside.

It's Spring now, my Jack-in-the box, and
you're taller. I've been watching just you
and your mother feeding. Are you and she
both rehearsing what has to come; your
distance from her further?

My Jack-in-the box, I learnt separation from
my children, acceptance of their steps and
stairs, the see-saw aches and empty arms
and when they grew enough to leave home,
that my seasons had folded inwards.
My Jack-in-the box,
I wish you family, joy and green grasses.

White elephant

Pressed together at my door
was a white elephant family;
skin crumpled and folded in
a discarded way: One limped
another had broken teeth,
its trunk squashed.

I didn't hesitate, asked them
inside; they squeezed and
shuffled around furniture,
glanced cautiously at my
umbrella stand.
Plenty of room I told them.

I made them all cups of tea,
though thought best not to
use the ivory handled cutlery.
I didn't ask how they'd come,
just mentioned that if it was
by boat, I thought them brave.

They didn't stay, but left me
some paper work to do. Their
goodbyes were flapping ears
and kind eyes. Perhaps others
will offer them an open door
and I'll see them on the news.

Welcome to my life

Come in
        I should tell you first there is no hope
        of a miracle here   there is no order, so don't be confused.
        Take notes if you like.

I imagine this living area stretches.
        Pretend you are circling or doing the Two-step –
        one forward   one back.

You will see   my once polished dining table's
        covered with books
        and dust plays hide and seek with them.
My chairs have attitude   they're not pleased
        they have to hold up my clothes.
They all dream of bottoms to feel needed,
        will be happy when I leave.

The wardrobe is filled with the past
        and my advice is not to open it –
        measure it if you like.

I'm sure you have noted   the display cabinet   TV
        radio   bookcases and computer.

Can you see the kitchen bench – my island?
        There, you can be the overseer.

It's in my bedroom where I unpack my life – it is cerebral hopscotch
        though it makes the wardrobe anxious –
        we've all got problems.

It's a good fit so please don't think op-shop.
Of course
        if you find a buyer today   you will have to give me
        plenty of time to pack...

The meanwhile living

They were the meanwhile living, concertinaed above the shopping centres, restaurants and parks, pursued by developers, chased up by pollution. Sky became their familiar. They were content until, in the higher and higher, they began to change. First, they lost their sense of smell, then their speech curled in on their tongues and all sentence ends fell off. In the higher and higher, their protruding eyes were sucked into blank screens, their ears disappeared, their jaws jangled and their pale faces wobbled like trophies on springs, until their bodies folded in on their bones. In their last days, passing asteroids became their tormentors and their blue sky faced off with space – the black of death, the silence of a last nursery rhyme. Their only legacy; broken lifts, rows of fractured balconies and empty windows that wept.

Loneliness

keeps my pace, day and night,
doesn't judge the failures I agonise over in my head;
sits me down and brings me a brandy if it's really bad
or a cup of tea, just for friendship;
checks my answer phone regularly, plays old songs,
is only quiet when I talk to a photograph;
takes my arm when I dress-up in my best, helps me
clip my necklace around my throat when my fingers can't,
wears the same perfume as me, keeps my pace;
goes with me to the shopping centre, holds my hand,
sometimes swings my bag over its shoulder
in a gesture of camaraderie;
encourages talking to mothers about their babies,
suggests I sit beside the man in the coffee shop,
thinks he looks lonely, picks a seat nearby, just in case,
gives me a thumbs-up when he smiles;
is generous if I'm invited out, suggests I stop over,
says it will stay at home, put its feet up.

The day my heart became a bird

Alone on the deck, in late afternoon,
with a second glass of wine, the colour of
blood, I hear my roses whispering, see
their green spikes pointing at my heart,
their leaves pirouetting.

I bend my head to look; blood trickles
across my clothes and shoes, crosses
the tiles in a thin, rhythmical line and
disappears over the edge; my grinning
roses, cheering it on.

I hear flapping, a metallic squeaking, feel
a squeezing across my ribs, a brushing of
light, a flash of colour, a blur flying from
my chest, over the roses
into Dusk.

What a performance.
The props: green and red paint,
backlighting, the roses as extras.
Clever Heart.

Soon

Old auntie, a loved large doll in a blue
nightdress, told me not to come back
again, that it's too late to talk about the
past, she's waiting to die.

So, I took her past with me for safe-
keeping: memories of gentle advice over
cups of milky tea, my little ones listening at
her feet to stories and songs.

Soon it will be my past that is left for safe-
keeping.

Old auntie told me she'd see me soon,
on that last day. I always trusted her
judgement but wish I'd asked her how
close soon was.

She's here again

She's here again –
that blond
twenty-year old
out on Friday night
smoking,
walking
in stockings
and high heels;

She's come to meet me,
as she always does,
when I return
to Circular Quay.

She folds my arm in hers,
walks me across old grey coat hanger
then up onto our favourite track
overlooking the beach
where we fished with him.

Salt breeze finds us,
and whisks us up to the Gap
where we watch rock and water
in conversation, rehearsing
a body snatch.

Fickle wind ferries us back to
the steps of bonneted Opera House,
and in the clatter of voices,
she asks if I want to go home.

I tell her it's not time yet,
that she'll be here again,
next time I return:
to ferry me home.

Polaroid

Sister, there you are, in a frozen pose,
standing on the snow; your red riding-
hood coat reporting the stillness; your
kind, penetrating eyes looking into
the distance of your life.

I was there that day, wearing aunty's
hand-knitted green and mauve beret,
preened in my new navy-blue jacket,
its silver buttons blinking the brittle
quietness.

I'd wanted to help you to find your
lost glove but you linked your hands
in feigned patience, pursed your lips,
refusing a bossy sister's fussing and
trying not to smile.

We were yet to be mothers, aunties,
grandmothers; were just a capture of
youth in a new Winter's playground,
hushed by its compacted silence.

Sister, soon I too, in a frozen pose,
will offer a gift of memory for each
that keep me: I too will look into
the distance of my life.

Mr Gusto

His 'Do-it-agains' ring in our ears,
and when he throws his voice, the walls vibrate.
If we ask him where his smile is,
it will creep across his face.

He likes to scare us sometimes; be a monster with claws
or a stomping dinosaur, swinging his arms; scrunching his
face up close to you with a gravelly voice, his fingers
splayed, his eyes rolling.

He will go *shopping* around the house, rattling old keys,
telling you they crunch; the colour and shape of his bag,
variously change. He drives *a car* with his arms held out,
turning at corners.

He might come to you from the kitchen with a packet
of dry macaroni and give you one, or have a metal bowl
on his head and you'll have to guess he is a bear,
of course.

He might sing on the phone if someone rings: either
Twinkle Star or *Happy Birthday,* or recite the
alphabet instead, several times; your patience will be
expected.

He might ask for your shoes when you sit down; will
walk around in them, tell you he is Dad. On your feet,
you could suddenly receive a running hug and must be
prepared to remain upright.

He likes to hop, spin and tumble, all at the same time. He
is joy and exhaustion in one. To get your attention, he'll
suddenly laugh and giggle at something you know is his
joke on you; rolling his eyes to draw you in.

He controlled the world he knew in those his whirl-wind days.

We called him Mr Gusto.

Hats

She steps onto the deck into the sun with a cup
of tea and honeyed toast on one of her mother's
antique plates. She's fussing over which hat
to wear to the funeral.

A hornet circles the plate, its buzzing
reminding her of a mother's honking car horn:
annoyance at waiting for a daughter to decide
which hat to wear to church; a daughter who
refuses to *parade* along that country church aisle.

She leaves the honeyed toast on the deck for
the hornet. If she had wings, she'd return
for one more Sunday, for the horn
to keep on honking.

She'll wear the hat that Susan gave her:
her mother would have approved the large bow.

Happiness

The elegant lady with red painted nails
sat next to me on the s-shaped seat by the doors
where winter slid in and out.

She rearranged her coat, caught my eye
and with a knowing smile, lifted happiness
from a small paper bag.

She handed it to me in its white serviette,
holding it lightly between thumb and finger.
It was still warm.

I thanked her and delicately wrapped
its wafting sweetness in my scarf.
Her kindness walked me home.

One room

You've already practiced ladling the past,
moving places, people, adventures, losses,
mistakes, into available head spaces, tacked
torn corners. You've been succinct, thinking
in shrinking allotments.

But who paces, spies through your keyhole?
Which will knock first, bring you a *one room*
only, to hold your unruly things, your loyal
shape-shifters? I know you won't be a no-sayer,
as befitting your age, but –

Be quick, re-sort *all* to folders. Add lists. Hide
books not yet read. Bridle your wall ghosts
into their frames. Don't forget the knick-knacks,
your history dates. You'll need to be secretive:
I know you're up to the challenge.

Visit after, *your one room*. Be a rifler for those
that hid, those that were forgotten or given as
gifts. Greedily day-dream. Obsess, a lot. Add
extensions to better show the old furniture,
properly made, the silver, antique crockery.

The others will visit, bring the old patterns
and colours... You have already practiced
moving your memories around, in your lap.
Be quick: Make copies. Back-up. Press Save.

Not alone

I am not alone.
I have a soul-mate, with me every day.
I tell her everything.
It can't be claimed by someone else
while I still have a mind.

I keep my soul-mate to myself, but
could tell others, if they ask, I am not alone.
I think her brain is esoteric,
has been floating in time:
I might have stolen it.

I opted out of a permanent visual image
or one revealed only in my dreams.
Though it might be nice if my soul-mate
could help me fold the sheets,
tease me when I cry in a movie.

Today the *al dente* spaghetti missed the bench,
made patterns on the floor; I nearly slipped.
Last week I found a bundle of books I'd kept.
It would be nice if my soul-mate and I
took turns reading them in bed.

I do get lonely sometimes.

Remember

Well,   I double-checked the taps and the stove
           and the sliding door before
               I left
and   just as I got to the door I turned around
           retraced my steps and double-
               checked again
and   well I left my mobile too
           in case I got hit by that car
               that just missed me yesterday
and   to leave a record of my voice for those
           that might want to hear
               it again
and   I took the phone off the cradle – well
           a burglar wouldn't know then
               if I was in or not
and   that is what I remembered about today
           before I left to go
               to the shops

Her rose

'I love you mother'
she said in a dream
when she visited me,
her rose
still in its vase
in her room.
'Are my brothers in?
Are their gardens grown?'
she asked, taking the rose.

She gave me flowers
she'd picked on the way –
then left to walk
in the rain
from my path to hers.

I'll wait for her to visit again.
I'll ask her brothers to water the roses.

Hands

Through her un-curtained window in morning's
shining, she watches a neighbour pushing a baby
in a shiny hooded pram, her delicate hands
resting on its handle.

She remembers her first baby in
a hand-me-down pram, the proud greediness
she'd felt for a gift of chattering life,
in those all-consuming days when milk
was love and responsibility and hands
did everything, without words.

In their silent midnights, hands mopped
floors, dreaming of hand-made dresses;
soaked the washing in the cold grey tub,
wrung it and lugged it outside in the early
mornings, hung it with wooden pegs.
If the house was lulled, clothes-line voices
escorted the hands inside, to stir the gluggy porridge.

Now, she guides her hands to the shelf
with the photo albums; begins with
the first: there's that indestructible pram,
her young hands!

Next

Bandages, crutches, wheelchairs and heads leaning against
imagined others, jumble the wait until "next" is called;
names shuffled and adjusted in a 'pack' of needs-must
where bloodied clothes are laundry responsibilities;
bandages declarations in white; all surfaces a stretched
web of hope:

      A heavy man folds into a chair like a child's toy.

      A loud bone-thin woman calls for someone to look
      after her black bag: "full from the pokies"

      A fully conscious shape-shifter strokes a woman's
      panting shoulders, pleading "Mum it's me!"

      A woman in a blue nightdress, cradling a bundle
      in a hospital blanket, whispers to the faces she passes bringing
      a cold breeze with her.

      A toddler – without words – standing on wobbly feet
      and splayed legs; his fingers opening and closing, his
      body turning like a spinning top; instructing us all.

      A tall, silver haired man across the aisle, clothed in
      striped pyjamas, grey slippers and mauve socks, rises
      in quiet majesty, makes one pivot turn, and sits down
      again.

      Two rowdy girls in pig-tails, pulling at their father's
      shirt sleeves, ask: "What happens next?"

Quietness descends for an answer we all want.

The gaps between

she too breathes slowly/ sits beside me/ near QVB's
glitter Christmas tree/ tells me she's going to the
Gap/ one more time/
is she the girl in the hostel?/ the girl that left the
short-sheeted beds/ teasers and beauties/ trailing a
blush/ suitcase and leather strap beside her/ leaving
the line-ups to matron's waiting/ matron's take the
lipstick off/ put the lipstick back/
I'm waiting for my daughter/ for our treat/
champagne and oysters/
she and I talk family/ she told me her daughter's
name/ the name of the girl in the hostel/ the gaps
between us/ my not asking/ a lingering/
is she the one who climbed the tree?/ the tree in
front of matron's room/
we all climbed through our dreams in the hostel/
through the gaps in our waiting/ waiting for life/
she's going to the top/ the Gap/ up rock steps/ past
bush shrubs acrid perfumes/ there where below/
rocks watch sea's flow/ its blue-green meeting/ its
returning ripples/ its rock and water conversations/
which rehearsing of a body snatch?/ which recording
of beauty and death?/ there where salt breeze/
finds body's blood/ she left quickly/ told me not to
wait too long for what I want/ I had no reply/ I
remember her name/ in the green and red felt city/
the tinsel/ a man is playing Jingle Bells on a drum and
beer bottles/ leaving QVB/ a voice/ let it go/...let it
go/...girl/

Tiny room

It's a tiny room with a single bed, two chairs and a round table with artificial flowers. There's also a chest of drawers, topped with family photos – she rearranges them if she is in the mood.

She has a gold rimmed card from the Queen; stores it in the bottom drawer with her calendars, tins of biscuits and thumbed *Woman's Weekly* featuring *"Eating at Home"*.

Each day, she dresses slowly, fusses over the right shoes and stockings; doesn't ask for help. She applies her make-up with care: first the powder-puff that smells of ball rooms and restaurants, then the red lipstick from the top drawer.

She checks her watch and takes the short walk down the corridor to a numbered table; leaves her walking stick behind. She pats down her dress as she sits alone; doesn't *see* the others, pretends there's only her.

She rubs the un-ironed table cloth between her fingers – misses the crocheted edges, a vase with a real flower and Mozart playing in the background. She doesn't eat.

She returns to her tiny room, sits on the unforgiving bed, stares at the family photos.

She's in a cage with an open door
she has no key for, to free herself.

Empty clothes-hangers

I know I have to live here.
I'd like a phone again.
I know I over did it before – all the calls.

I learnt my lesson.
I'd ring just once a week now
if I had a phone.

I've lost my friends.
Where is my daughter?

I'd like to go shopping...
I think I need more nylons.
I might want a summer nightdress...
I'll shout you lunch...

I don't like you *doing* my clothes.
Oh, well... And thank you.
You'll bring them back?

Who is he in the photograph?
Did I marry again?

It's hot in here – the rhythm of clothes...
The coat hangers dancing around...
I have to leave.

White

she held the white lady
the white lady held her...

had the white lady
lived with welts
that were mountains she could conquer?
tasted her tears
that cleansed the flattened bed?
learnt to stiffen her wounds
to stand up and speak for themselves?
known a scream
was someone else's pain?
had an honest mirror
to show her no fear?
told herself
a punch was just a bruise of colours?
found a place of red
where she could break rules?
counted her days backwards
to find her before self?

she held the white lady
the white lady held her...

Dew-drop whispering

I bathe her stiff body.
Her little face and neck
lift towards me.

Her eyes towards me,
her tiny voice asks
'Is that you?'

Gently I roll her from
side to side, as if rocking
a child.

I think I hear
The lord's prayer,
a dew-drop whispering.

I wait for her
to say goodnight, tuck me in,
kiss my cheek.

Little face frightened

You frightened you'll fall
You little face frightened.

You rage
when they pick you up
to put you back in bed.

You rage from the chair
they keep you in,
a feeding tray across
to trap you.

You busy sorting
things across the room.

You little yell at them,
'Look at my things!
I'm busy,
leave me alone.'

You are alone.

Loss of her

I sit beside her, penned in her babble words.
I listen for old whispers of us;
hope to hear my name, but accept
the absence of it, rather than walk away.

She takes the gloves out of her old black
bag, puts them back in: one white and two
brown. Could a past lover have the other
white?

Her wagging finger points along the skirting board.
I think she's counting shoes;
Life is short... Buy the shoes...
I'm sure she said that once.

She whispers, turns her head, her eyes
sweeping the room. What is she telling someone?
Again she takes out the gloves, stares at me,
asks 'Do I know you?'

It is too late for an answer or story
about the missing glove.
I'll have to invent memories
for the time we still have together.

Holding places

You, in lamp's yellow – a small
sun – your first holding place.

You, escaping the white lace exit,
bringing us your rainbow palette.

You, concaving me in you, taking me
past the focal point,
refracting light, finding angles.

You honeycombing holding places
for each of us, where we can hear
your laughter.

You: a daughter,
sister, wife,
mother.

Your turn

White Gum, arms held high in pride, you've
welcomed clasping spider webs and nature's
parachutes; the hugs of familial corsets of
orange, brown and black, and been grateful
too that bark has kept the soft of you.

You've watched the generations, standing
outside their home, listened to their voices
and stories through openings and cracks;
some days, bent to see through its windows
with your confidant wind.

You've watched the two girls grow, kept
a memory of the first time you held them in
your arms, seen them waiting for their
father on hair-wash Sundays, heard old
fireplace's laments.

White Gum, you knew your day would
come: You've seen the others take their
turn. Today the two women will hold
you in their arms; walk you to the fire,
your confidant wind, sing you.

waiting

green leaves whisper through small window's waiting/
cream blinds sway/ your shadow is in my tiny room again/

you are in your army uniform/ waiting at the gate/ to drive
me to the Saturday night dance/ in the old church hall/ we
pass the peanut farms/ macadamia trees/ ocean our distant
chaperone/ we are shy/ talk to the window screen/

our first dance the waltz/ our last the jive/ our first kiss
that night/

I can still see the faces of the children we didn't have/ the
boy kicking a football/ the girl in the floral dress I made
for her/

I sometimes think I see you stirring a sugary cup of tea/
your crooked smile/ hear you calling my name to walk with
you/ tell me we'll grow old together/

listen! / corridor voices/ march of flat shoes/ if you wait/ I'll
go with you/ I'm ready/

Light

Your eyelids in early morning sunlight
slit-opened, harvesting light
shining a path along a trellis of flowers
for the smile you'd always given,
for the words
we needed to say to you.

We placed our silent memories before you,
wanted to believe you were listening,
kissed your still warm forehead,
heard your rising and falling laugh
echo in our past.

We were your witnesses.
Said goodbye - not wanting to,
helped you through that door
to return to your life's star;
to walk in its light.

Then and now

Once you told me
you liked my perfume
Once you brought me
a bottle of expensive red wine
Once you said
we would have coffee each morning
Once you reminded me
you'd ring each day if we were apart

These days
If you bring me perfume
I will put it in my mouth
If you bring a bottle of wine
I will try to catch its reflections
If you bring me coffee
I will dip my fingers in

Don't come back tomorrow
I won't remember you

Acknowledgements

Janette would like to thank and acknowledge the development and editorial work of renown poet: Melinda Smith in 2018, as well as editorial support from local author: Mike Pieloor

About the Author

Janette Pieloor is an established Australian poet with more than 30 years of publications in Australian poetry anthologies, magazines and journals, including in The Best Australian Poems and The Australian Poetry Journal.

Janette has 4 grown children and 4 grandchildren and lives in Canberra. She is an active member of the New Territory Poets and the U3A ACT Poetry Groups.

In 2015, Walleah Press published Janette's first poetry collection: RIPPLES UNDER THE SKIN

2019 Editions
Palace of Memory: An elegy **Paul Hetherington**
Acting Like a Girl **Sandra Renew**
A Coat of Ashes **Jackson**
Summer Haiku **Owen Bullock**
A Common Garment **Anita Patel**
Giant Steps **Various**
Some Sketchy Notes on Matter **Angela Gardner**
Wardrobe of Selves **Peter Bakowski**
Breathing in Stormy Seasons **Stephanie Green**
Strange Creatures **Alyson Miller**

2018 Editions
The Uncommon Feast **Eileen Chong**
Inlandia **KA Nelson**
Peripheral Vision **Martin Dolan**
The Love of the Sun **Matt Hetherington**
Moving Targets **Jen Webb**
Things I Have Thought to Tell You Since I Saw You Last **Penelope Layland**
The Many Uses of Mint **Ravi Shankar**
Abstractions **Various**
ACE: Arresting, Contemporary stories by Emerging Writers **Various**

all titles available from
www.recentworkpress.com

RECENT
WORK
PRESS

CPSIA information can be obtained
at www.ICGtesting.com
Printed in the USA
LVHW040119121119
637080LV00006B/915/P